CHAKRAS

An Introductory Guide To Chakras: Unlocking The Third Eye, Cultivating A Strong Aura, And Enhancing Body Healing Through Meditation Techniques And The Harnessing Of Positive Energies

Erik Butler

TABLE OF CONTENT

The Chakras 1

The Role Of The Crown Chakra In Regulating Energy Currents 10

The Second Chakra 22

Awakening The Kundalini Shakti 32

How Do Chakra Points Work? 37

The Fundamental Chakra For Earthly Stability 48

Chakras And Science 63

The Seven Chakras 82

Chakra Mudras 91

Chakra Energy Flow Maintenance 98

Reestablishing Balance In The Third Eye Chakra 109

Comprehending The Fundamentals Of Your Energetic Chakras 116

An Elucidation On The 7 Primary Chakras 144

The Chakras

Previously, you may not have correlated the harnessing of your chakra energy with the practice of meditation, yet it indeed holds significant relevance. The intellect, physical form, and essence harmonize as a singular entity via the chakras. The chakras represent the focal points of transcendental energy within the human body. They represent the focal points of energy that lie in alignment with the vertebral column. This illustration displays the precise locations within the body where each chakra is traditionally believed to reside. Hence, it is imperative to observe proper posture during the practice of meditation.

Every chakra possesses distinctive attributes and conveys heterogeneous significance. Progressing from the base chakra to the crown chakra, we shall delineate the symbolic significance and corresponding hues of each individual chakra.

The Root Chakra profoundly influences the sensation of being firmly rooted and the instinctual mechanisms for ensuring survival. It is intertwined with the physiological response known as the fight or flight reaction. The hue that is linked with the fundamental chakra is the color red.

The succeeding chakra in line is the Sacral Chakra. The sacral chakra exerts influence over aspects such as sexuality, bliss, and longing. Furthermore, it is linked to one's aptitude for innovation and the capacity to exhibit empathy towards others. The hue typically linked to the sacral chakra is orangish in nature.

Next, we encounter the Solar Plexus Chakra. The solar plexus chakra is responsible for fostering a sense of confidence and fostering respect towards oneself and others. This energy center is recognized for its role in fostering both personal and professional achievements. The hue linked to this particular chakra is yellow.

The subsequent element is the Heart Chakra, which governs one's capacity for affection and exerts an impact on interpersonal connections. Damaging a relationship through the expression of anger, envy, or distrust may be indicative of an imbalance in the heart chakra. The hue commonly linked to the heart chakra is green.

The Throat Chakra pertains to your capacity to articulate and convey your thoughts and feelings. This specific chakra has the potential to influence the individual's capacity to articulate their emotions and convey veracity. The hue that is typically linked to the throat chakra is blue.

The Third Eye Chakra serves as the source of intuition and inspirational thought. This particular energy center known as the chakra facilitates the enhancement of your capacity to attentively concentrate and perceive the broader perspective. The hue traditionally linked to the third eye chakra is indigo.

The ultimate chakra is the Crown Chakra, serving as the focal point for transcendence and enlightenment. This particular chakra symbolizes your aptitude for spiritual connectivity. The hue connected with the crown chakra is violet or purple.

It is imperative to comprehend the pivotal significance of the chakras in dictating the flux of energy within oneself. The presence of obstructed energy in any of these domains may contribute to both physical ailments and a sense of discontentment. The process of enhancing and revitalizing the chakras is known to contribute to the harmonization of various aspects of one's existence.

The second chakra, known as Svadhisthana

Il secondo chakra viene denominato Svadhisthana, con il significato di "soffermare su se stessi", poiché è intimamente correlato alla sfera emotiva.

Il secondo chakra è caratterizzato dal colore arancione, il quale rappresenta il senso del gusto.

Il simbolo di Svadhisthana consiste in un fiore di loto di colore arancione con sei delicate corolle.

La localizzazione si trova in prossimità degli organi genitali, più specificamente nella regione compresa tra i genitali e l'ombelico. I nervi convergono per formare un gruppo distintivo e altamente sensibile chiamato plesso sacrale. Svadhisthana presides over bodily functions that are inherently connected to fluids, such as circulation, urine elimination, reproduction, and fertility. Accordingly, its associated element is water, and it is strongly linked to the moon, which governs earthly waters. L'animale associato è il coccodrillo, che dimora nelle acque fluviali e lacustri, mentre come opzione alternativa si possono considerare gli esemplari della fauna marina in generale.

Contrary to the first chakra, which represents stability and grounding, encompassing all that is solid - hence its association with the earth element - the second chakra embodies the concept of transformation, fluidity, and continual change. La sessualità, il desiderio e l'impulso riproduttivo sono connessi ad esso.

"The mantra associated with the second chakra is vam." (formal tone)

Gli apparati coinvolti sono, naturalmente, l'apparato genitale, i testicoli e le ovaie, nonché le estremità superiori. Questo chakra riveste un'importanza di notevole rilievo per i professionisti creativi che si dedicano all'arte manuale e che, attraverso il loro processo creativo, coinvolgono attivamente il corpo, come ad esempio ballerini, pittori, scultori e attori. Le problematiche a questo livello causano incongruenze nella capacità riproduttiva e una ridotta fertilità, oltre a generare disturbi sessuali come ipo o iperattività del desiderio, nonché relazioni amorose poco gratificanti. Allacciata a un blocco potrebbe manifestarsi anche una correlazione, come ad esempio un legame con l'abuso di alcol o di altre sostanze stupefacenti, o potrebbero essere presenti eventuali disfunzioni renali o cardiovascolari, problemi nel ciclo mestruale (si tratta sempre di questioni inerenti ai fluidi corporei). Un blocco potrebbe altresì indicare la presenza di eventi traumatici nell'infanzia o di traumi emotivi non ancora elaborati. Dal punto di vista emotivo, se il corretto funzionamento del secondo chakra viene garantito, le emozioni scorrono liberamente, comprese quelle che potrebbero essere considerate negative, non causando alcun tipo di conflitto o conseguenza indesiderata. Qualora emergano difficoltà di equilibrio, è possibile che le emozioni vengano sopite o siano causa di disagi.

The Role Of The Crown Chakra In Regulating Energy Currents

The Crown Chakra, also known as Sahasrara, is associated with the pineal gland; however, it is often symbolized as being situated slightly above the top of the head in various frameworks. It harnesses celestial energy, serves as a wellspring of motivation, and establishes a profound bond between one's individual being and the vastness of the cosmos. The capacity to perceive that subtle, subdued inner voice, which guides us towards the ideal state of affairs and directs us on how to harmoniously collaborate with them.

Envision, if you will, a meticulously traced trajectory from the fundamental energy center known as the Root Chakra, Muladhara, ascending seamlessly through the aforementioned interceding chakras, ultimately converging with Shahasrara, the esteemed Crown Chakra. This constitutes the primary energy trajectory, establishing an ongoing energy interchange that traverses from the base to the apex, subsequently reversing course. However, it is not the sole option available.

Two additional energy loops traverse in opposite directions, intersecting repeatedly along this central axis. These entities are occasionally portrayed as a duo of serpents, with their tails connected to the Root Chakra and their heads terminating at the Brow Chakra. The Crown Chakra is portrayed as a set of wings ascending beyond the top of the head. Please take a moment to contemplate a medical caduceus, wherein two serpents are entwined around a central pole, while wings adorn its upper portion. The resemblance is not coincidental.

For optimal functioning of all the chakras, it is imperative that each one achieves equilibrium, allowing the energy to manifest harmoniously in a smooth and unimpeded manner as it transitions seamlessly from one center to another, effortlessly traversing through all the intricate pathways.

Should any chakra, singularly or collectively, become imbalanced, the resulting outcome entails the accumulated stagnation or excessive rapid movement of energy within. When this phenomenon transpires, the resulting inequity will materialize in the tangible realm as somatic or psychological disorders.

These may not be of excellent quality. They may manifest as an individual who experiences discomfort in social gatherings or as someone who consumes sweets in secret while publicly expressing remorse over weight gain. Graver disparities may become evident through the onset of illnesses or medical ailments. Alternatively, it is possible for the imbalance to be caused by medical conditions or diseases.

How does one go about achieving equilibrium among the different chakras? There exist numerous methods. However, one of the most straightforward and advantageous techniques is referred to as grounding and centering. If feasible, it is recommended to keep your footwear aside and stand on the ground for this practice. However, it is adaptable to any location and can be conducted at any given moment. Unless the practitioner deliberately draws attention to it, it is unlikely to be noticed by anyone. The aforementioned task becomes somewhat challenging when performed within a relocating vehicle.

Establishing Stability and Focus: Envision extending roots from the foundational point of your spine, extending through your lower limbs, and traversing through your feet to penetrate the depths of the earth. If you happen to reside in an apartment building or a comparable edifice, envision the roots extending themselves deep within the infrastructure, ultimately penetrating the Earth's soil.

It harnesses the vitality of our planet, drawing it upwards through the spiraling pathways of the serpentine channels, eventually reaching the brow chakra. In this instance, the energy is mutually transferred or transformed (depending on the requirement) by means of contact with the crown chakra, subsequently propelled downwards along the central channel towards the root chakra.

As the terrestrial energies traverse each respective focal point, they accumulate miscellaneous fragments of energy in their trajectory. They resolve and harmonize challenges, such as a conflict with a cherished individual or an ambiguity regarding the success of a venture. This procedure, in and of itself, will not serve as a definitive solution to the problem; however, it will facilitate coherent deliberation. It may not yield clarification upon the initial repetition, perhaps not even after the repetition has occurred several hundred times. In due time, with diligent practice, it will facilitate the achievement of center balance.

On occasion, when an individual has undergone significant life-altering experiences such as illness or the unfortunate passing of a cherished individual, more robust approaches may be necessary to restore equilibrium to a specific chakra. Alternatively, it could be the case that the utilization of the energies associated with a specific chakra is indispensable within the context of a given circumstance or objective. The forthcoming chapter will center upon this subject matter.

The Second Chakra

The Sacral chakra serves as the focal point for your creative expression. The reason for its name is derived from its positioning at the sacrum. It is alternatively referred to as swadhisthana.

This particular chakra pertains to an individual's artistic expression and fervor. Furthermore, this energy center serves as the focal point for cultivating artistic expressions, maintaining a household, engaging in entrepreneurial endeavors, and other aspects of our lives wherein our creative abilities can be deployed. It also encompasses sensuality, interpersonal connections, purity, vulnerability, and our interactions with individuals and the world at large.

Due to its close proximity to the genital region, the Sacral chakra also governs matters pertaining to sexuality, enjoyment, and procreation. In the event that the swadhisthana exhibits prominent energy, one shall display a tendency towards seeking pleasure. Not necessarily an individual who finds pleasure in matters of sexuality and interpersonal connections. Furthermore, one has the capacity to derive pleasure from any other entity found within the realms of existence that has the ability to impart joy. To reiterate, you are an individual who desires to derive pleasure from the experiences of this world.

An inherent attribute of an individual possessing a predominant Sacral chakra is their inclination towards experiencing life with heightened intensity when compared to those who exhibit dominance in other chakras, notably the

Root chakra. When your Sacral chakra is predominant, you experience life with a heightened intensity. As the intensity level escalates, the capacity to perceive diverse facets of existence transitions from one domain to another.

Guilt serves as an obstruction to the proper functioning of the Sacral chakra. Additionally, it demonstrates signs of fear, disgust, remorse, jealousy, and shame. Some of the somatic symptoms associated with an obstructed swadhisthana include discomfort in the lumbar region, urinary difficulties, complications related to the uterus, diminished libido, and erectile dysfunction.

Conduct introspection and ascertain the entirety of the culpability that weighs upon your conscience. Consider all the things for which you hold yourself responsible. Then stop. Cease attributing any wrongdoing or mishaps to yourself. You must come to terms with the truth. These things happen. Ensure that guilt does not obscure and taint your vitality. In order to exert a positive influence on the world, it is imperative that you grant yourself forgiveness. Relinquish any sense of blame and guilt harbored within yourself.

It is indeed attainable to awaken the Sacral chakra by means of meditative practices. Adopt the kneeling stance, then gradually descend by resting your body on the posterior side of your legs. Please position your hands on your lap, palms facing upwards, oriented towards each other, and with the right hand resting above the left. The tip of the thumbs should touch each other. Kindly, gently close your eyes and allow your mind to come to a state of stillness. Direct your attention to the positioning of the energy hub. During the course of this activity, conjure a mental image of a vibrant, spherical manifestation of energy resembling an orange hue. Allow this sphere to heighten in intensity as it permeates every fiber of your being. Utter the phonetic utterance "VAM" in tandem with the vocalization of the cognitive affirmation, "I possess the attribute of being creative."

Regarding physical exercises to stimulate the chakra, one can engage in specific yoga postures that focus on the lower abdominal region. Exercises designed to facilitate hip opening can also be beneficial. Please remember to perform your sun salutations. They promote a dynamic range of motions that serve to stimulate both your artistic expression and sensual awareness. Engage in dancing without being conscious of onlookers. Undoubtedly, you have encountered that statement previously. It serves as an excellent method for initiating the activation of the sacral chakra.

If you prefer a more relaxed approach to unblocking your swadhisthana, you may consider indulging in a soothing massage or spending an evening immersed in the viewing of films that evoke sensuality or sorrow. Engage in this action while dispersing orange oil extract using the oil burner.

The Root Chakra (Muladhara)

This is the primary energy center, situated at the lowermost part of the spinal column in the coccyx region within the human anatomy. The color red carries implicit symbolism and is associated with our interpersonal and familial bonds, our connection to the tangible aspects of the Earth, our innate survival instincts and senses of stability, as well as the experience of gratification. The foundational aspect of the root chakra symbolizes our grounding and rootedness; as a result, the element associated with it is earth. The primary focus lies in the aspects of sustaining existence, ensuring stability, safeguarding oneself, and establishing a foundation for nourishment. It serves as the embodiment of terrestrial stabilizing energy due to its proximity to the Earth. Frequently, it is emblemized by a quadrilateral shape and associated with the olfactory sense, with coral serving as the designated gemstone and Mars being the celestial body chosen to symbolize it. The crown chakra is associated with its corresponding spiral pair.

The root chakra serves as the locus of physical energy and the intrinsic instinct for survival in the human species. In general, the root chakra serves as the fundamental foundation for human beings, governing their physical survival, vitality, and sense of security. If the vitality of this energy center is harmoniously activated within you, sensations of being firmly anchored and fortified envelop your being. You perceive oneself as having ample room in every aspect of your life and exude a resilient and unwavering aura.

Individuals who possess an abundance of this chakra tend to exhibit an inclination towards possessiveness, materialism, a strong preoccupation with personal security, resistance to change, and occasionally, a proclivity for greed. Conversely, in the event of a deficiency, one may exhibit symptoms of anxiety, apprehension, and a lack of stability or rootedness, potentially leading to a state of homelessness. It is probable that you might experience feelings of insecurity and frustration with regards to your belongings.

The fundamental requirements for sustenance, protection, and well-being derive from this chakra, as it pertains to our connection with the natural world, enabling us to establish a solid grounding in our earthly existence. If one ever requires the manifestation of objectives within the physical realm, be it in matters of commerce or acquisition of material wealth, then it is imperative to direct one's focus towards this specific chakra as an energy source, so as to achieve triumph.

The base chakra is linked to the subsequent anatomical regions: pelvis, lower extremities, lumbar spine, and reproductive organs. The male sexual organs predominantly reside within the first chakra, thereby resulting in a corporeal manifestation of male sexual energy. In the case of a female, her primary sexual organs are situated within the second chakra, hence, the experience of female sexual energy takes on an emotional nature. The chakras in question are both associated with and connected to the flow of sexual energy.

The fundamental chakra is linked to matters of the emotions, such as irrational fears and phobias, as well as financial concerns encompassing wealth and reproductive difficulties. Furthermore, it is correlated with ailments such as intestinal obstruction, gastrointestinal disturbances, urinary tract inflammations, and diminished blood circulation leading to cold extremities. An extensive understanding of the fundamental chakra will bestow upon you the sagacity and illumination to grasp the interconnectedness of all things, and endow you with the capacity to confront ambiguity and maintain a state of stability.

Awakening The Kundalini Shakti

The pursuit of spiritual growth commences from its very foundation. The Muladhara Chakra, alternatively referred to as the Root Chakra, can be found positioned at the base of the spinal column. It assists us in conquering our apprehensions and cultivating our innate survival instincts. With the activation of the Muladhara Chakra, our olfactory and auditory perception is heightened, enabling us to discern the mental and emotional states of those in our vicinity.

What precisely is the fundamental underlying factor responsible for the discord prevalent in our present circumstances? The solution to this inquiry resides in the conviction that we shall unfailingly harvest the consequences of our previous actions. It is imperative that we acknowledge the errors we have made, whether purposefully or inadvertently, either in our present existence or in past incarnations. The cause of our present state of happiness or sorrow can be attributed to our past actions, or Karma. Undoubtedly, we have also contributed significantly to positive outcomes, resulting in our existence being comprised of a blend of contradictory thoughts and emotions. In a fleeting moment, existence embodies pure bliss, only to swiftly transition into a deep yearning to discern the precise juncture at which our lives took an unfortunate turn. All of these experiences are repressed within this Chakra. It is imperative that we address the truth in order to cultivate the inherent qualities ingrained within our consciousness. To accomplish this, it is necessary to activate the latent Kundalini Shakti residing within this particular Chakra.

Upon the activation of the Muladhara Chakra, we initially encounter the complete intensity of our unrestrained emotions. We have relinquished the accumulated anger, suppressed apprehension, intense distress, and hidden inner turmoil, thus preparing ourselves to embrace the thoroughly liberating emotions of tranquility, serenity, peace, and bliss. Our belief in a higher power is revitalized as we grasp the essence of our existence and begin perceiving it through a fresh lens.

Useful Practices:

The most straightforward and secure approach to rouse this inactive spiritual energy is through the repetitive recitation of the mantra LAM, which is specifically linked to this particular chakra. Reciting this mantra alleviates built-up tension, promoting a deep state of relaxation.

The Muladhara Chakra is correlated with the hue of red. Incorporating a greater amount of the color red into our attire will engender a heightened sense of confidence, enabling us to confront and ultimately prevail over our apprehensions and vulnerabilities. The crystals noted for their ability to enhance our confidence include Garnets, Quartz, Red Jasper, and Haematite.

Reflecting upon our previous deeds during our periods of meditation will yield dual benefits. Initially, we shall draw upon our resilience and determination, taking inspiration from the cherished recollections of our history. The profound joy and serenity that we encountered during that period will empower us to confront our emotions of apprehension, disgrace, and animosity, thereby guaranteeing our ultimate liberation from them.

The Kriya Yoga practice, the Mahamudra technique, as well as the Ashwini and Manduki Mudras, are all highly efficacious exercises known to stimulate the activation of this particular Chakra. These exercises unlock the Kundalini shakti as we are elevated from a state of ignorance to a plane of consciousness.

How Do Chakra Points Work?

The phrase 'Chakra Points or Chakras' has witnessed a notable surge in usage during recent years, being referenced in various forms of media, television programs, and extensively across multiple social networking platforms. In addition to a fundamental comprehension, numerous individuals lack familiarity regarding the implications and personal relevance of these terms. The mastery of harnessing one's Chakras is a teachable skill accessible to all individuals, and through diligent training, the proper utilization of these vital conduits has the potential to enhance one's holistic well-being, encompassing both the physical and mental aspects.

There are numerous Chakra points dispersed throughout the entirety of your body, the primary ones being vertically aligned from your pelvis to the crown of your head. Energy emanates from the primary Chakras and extends towards the subordinate Chakras, akin to the intricate network of veins found on botanical foliage. If there is a balanced and controlled flow of energy through the primary Chakras, the minor energy points will remain well-maintained without any need for your active intervention.

What precisely does the term 'Chakra Point' denote?

A chakra point signifies a conduit through which the inherent energy of the cosmos, commonly referred to as prana or life force, permeates and traverses your corporeal, cognitive, and metaphysical being. They serve as the conduits through which you exert influence over the flow of energy within your body, facilitating the equilibrium and regulation of the various physiological processes governed by each point.

Every aspect of your physiological functions, ranging from cardiovascular activity, cognitive processes, reproductive capabilities, intellectual operations, neural operations, and the entirety of bodily functions, are intricately linked to these channels of energy. Furthermore, all of these functions can be significantly influenced by the regulation and manipulation of the energy that permeates through these channels.

The flow of Prana continuously traverses the Chakras in your body, nourishing it with innate energy. This energy consists of discrete currents, known as Nadis, which together constitute a cohesive flow of energy referred to as the Sushumna. Meditators from the Eastern traditions have ascertained that, at any given moment, a network of up to 72 thousand Nadis is observed coursing through the Chakra points within the body.

Sushumna is considered as the primary channel through which energy flows, connecting the base Chakra to the Crown Chakra in a vertical pathway.

The Pingala Nadi is one of the two streams of energy channels, also known as Nadis. The Pingala represents a thermogenic current connected with solar and masculine energies, governing the functionalities of the right side of the body and mind.

Ida Nadi refers to the second stream of the Nadi system. A serene current that aligns with the lunar essence and encompasses all elements tied to feminine forces, exerting influence over the left side of the body and intellect.

The state of equilibrium and fluidity in the Sushumna pathway has a direct impact on your well-being and capabilities, which are regulated through the utilization of your seven primary Chakra centers. By facilitating the proper maintenance of prana's flow through these seven primary access points, one can cultivate an optimal flow through the secondary Chakras, resulting in the acquisition of the advantages associated with a harmonized energy system.

Similarly to how arteries can experience occlusion or obstruction, the Chakra points within your body can also undergo blockages or disruptions. Blocked chakras will not only diminish the inherent flow of energy within the body, but will also result in a sluggish and nearly stagnant flow in certain regions.

Consider the sensations experienced when there is inadequate circulation to the hand or foot; numbness, discomfort, and impaired motor function will ensue. This is the same with our Chakras; a broken or slow prana flow leads to health problems and instability in our physical, mental and spiritual being.

Multiple factors can contribute to the occurrence of blockages, with negative emotions frequently identified as one of the primary instigators. It is unnecessary for you to contribute to this negativity, as the prana is interconnected with the universal life force. The negativity emitted by individuals in your vicinity can be assimilated through our Sushumna. Acquiring the skill of regulating and preserving the flow of energy within yourself through the process of purifying the Chakras and eliminating any obstructions that may exist will enable you to reinstate the innate equilibrium of your Prana.

Acquiring proficiency in the activation and deactivation of your Chakras may require diligent efforts, particularly if you lack prior experience in this endeavor. Nevertheless, similar to any endeavor, the task becomes progressively simpler with practice, ultimately transforming into a seamless and effortless skill, allowing you to effortlessly manipulate the opening and closing of doors at your discretion, showcasing your proficiency.

Your vital life force transcends the confines of your physical body. The vital force courses through the internal pathways, radiating outward to create an external circuit and a protective energy field surrounding the physique, only to ultimately return to its intrinsic course. Assuming that there are no hindrances within the 7 primary Chakras, the flow of prana can be consistently circulated along the Sushumna pathway. The intensity at which this energy moves through your Chakras can be determined as you initiate and conclude their activation.

The Aura, often designated as the external prana flow, alongside the physical prana, constitutes the two most commonly alluded to components among the four primary levels of energy.

The Solar Plexus Chakra, also known as the Third Chakra.

The solar plexus chakra is intricately linked to our perception of personal strength, our capacity to exude self-assurance, and our aptitude for managing our own destiny. The energy is characterized by the hues Amber or yellow in color. The chakra in question is closely intertwined with our self-assurance, self-respect, and self-value. This energy is situated within the region extending from the naval area to the breastbone. This constitutes your inherent potential and can be accessed in instances where critical choices are at stake, moments of diminished self-assurance, or the need to amicably settle disputes arise.

There exists a delicate equilibrium in the utilization of authority. To illustrate, there exists an approach to convey one's opinions confidently without exploiting authority, exhibiting aggressive behavior, or acting self-centeredly. This represents a force that empowers us to uphold our convictions and embrace our true identities. It facilitates the equilibrium between morality and immorality, and showcases our inherent value when we engage in such actions. If there is an imbalance in this particular facet of your life, it is possible that you might exhibit excessive competitiveness. There exist various means by which power can be misused and individuals may engage in excessive self-aggrandizement, thereby allowing their egos to dominate our existence. If you consistently exhibit a tendency to be inflexibly correct, it is possible that there is a chakra in need of purification pertaining to this aspect of your personality. This should not be interpreted as advocating for passivity in the face of mistreatment, but rather emphasizes the importance of maintaining a delicate equilibrium between asserting one's authority and maintaining meaningful connections with others.

Certain individuals require a perpetual surge of adrenaline to experience a sense of empowerment, or they feel compelled to belittle others, which signifies an excessive exercise of their authority. Through attaining inner clarity and comprehending the essence of your integrity and values, you will enhance your ability to engage with this energy. Consequently, you will no longer adopt a defensive stance but rather possess the capacity to protect yourself when the need arises.

Gaining a comprehensive comprehension of one's own identity bestows a sense of empowerment. By harmonizing this particular chakra, individuals can attain a deeper clarity regarding their true selves and their personal convictions. Freedom can be found in the unmitigated expression of one's authentic self and the inner strength to steadfastly embrace one's identity amidst the complexities of this existence. During moments of excessive stress or a perceived inability to accomplish a task, one can resort to channeling the energy within their solar plexus chakra. This energy represents your individual power reservoir and epitomizes the inherent strength you possess.

Ways to balance

The Manipura, also known as the naval chakra, can achieve balance through the practice of boat pose in yoga.

By achieving equilibrium between authority and personal integrity, refraining from adopting a defensive stance, and forging a connection with the essence of power, and accepting it rather than opposing it, you will discover your equilibrium. Through the cultivation of this specific chakra, one can effectively harness their latent potential and effectively address apprehensions related to venturing into uncertain territories and lacking self-confidence. You will instill the necessary sense of assurance and self-assurance to effectively engage and pursue opportunities, while also cultivating personal discipline. In the event of being obstructed, an individual may manifest signs of diminished self-esteem, a sense of stagnation, and a dearth of courage.

Equilibrium is achieved through a cognitive comprehension of one's own self. An additional aspect of cultivating a symbiotic bond with this energy manifests through heeding your intuition or innate instincts. This sensation arises as a result of the energy within your power source chakra and warrants diligent attention rather than dismissal.

The Fundamental Chakra For Earthly Stability

The root chakra is widely regarded as the foremost among the seven chakras, primarily due to its strong association with the physical realm. In such instances, participating in endeavors that foster mindfulness of one's physical self proves to be an efficacious approach towards fortifying this chakra. The incorporation of activities such as walking, engaging in sports, practicing martial arts, participating in yoga, and engaging in tai chi has been demonstrated to be conducive to the achievement of this objective. Engaging in routine domestic tasks such as dishwashing, household cleaning, or car maintenance can yield significant advantages. Nonetheless, engaging in activities that result in desensitization or reduced tolerance to pain is discouraged. Engagement in physical activity is highly encouraged to promote the well-being of the root chakra, yet excessive fatigue is strictly advised against.

The sacral chakra is situated in the pelvic region, specifically at the foundation of the spine. The chakra in question is influenced by various factors such as the hue red, the terrestrial constituent, and the olfactory perception.

The sound it emits corresponds to the musical note C. Gemstones suitable for the initial chakra encompass garnet, ruby, red coral, bloodstone, agate, and red jasper. The bodily organs and systems influenced by the root chakra encompass the bladder, prostate gland, lower limbs, excretory system, adrenal glands, dental structures, kidneys, large intestine, circulatory system, and skeletal framework. It is also impacted by concerns related to weight.

Situated at its foundation, the root chakra exerts influence over the physical body's most elemental frequency. It addresses and encompasses distinctive matters pertaining to personal identity, physical well-being, safeguarding, protection, accumulation of resources, and reproductive instincts. The foundational chakra facilitates the establishment of a grounded and harmonious connection between individuals and the earth. Providing the bedrock for our complete chakra energy system, the sacral chakra assumes the role of the foundational chakra.

Opening the Root Chakra

By engaging in the practice of meditation, one can initiate the activation of their foundational chakra. To commence, allow the index finger to make contact with the tips of the thumb. In order to activate the base chakra, one must concentrate on its specific location. That refers to the area located between the anal orifice and the reproductive organs. Now, it is necessary for you to execute a rudimentary incantation incorporating the phonetic element LAM.

The Advantages Derived from Attaining Equilibrium in the Root Chakra

Individuals who possess harmonious energy in their root chakra tend to exhibit a state of good health and stability. They exude vibrancy and demonstrate remarkable vigor. They embrace their incarnation. These individuals possess the knowledge and ability to maintain and nurture their physical well-being.

What are the Consequences of an Excessive Energy Imbalance in the Root Chakra?

Although an inadequate level of root chakra energy is undesirable, an excessive amount of root chakra energy may also prove detrimental. Individuals exhibiting an abundance of energy in their root chakra frequently display traits of egotism. They commonly exhibit an abundance of sexual vigor, making them susceptible to succumbing and fixating on carnal gratification. They demonstrate an excessive preoccupation with indulgence, thereby neglecting the importance of emotional bonding.

Their opinions are biased. These individuals have a tendency to exhibit a judgmental and domineering nature. They possess an innate compulsion to maintain control. They demonstrate a strong attachment to wealth and material possessions.

The effects of a diminished energy level in the root chakra

Individuals who possess deficient energy in their root chakra exhibit a complete contrast to those who have an excess of energy in the same chakra. That is to say, they exhibit a propensity for low self-confidence or a complete absence thereof. They exhibit no interest in engaging in sexual activities. Additionally, they often experience a sense of being unloved and perceive themselves as incapable of receiving love.

At the most minimal level of energy within the root chakra, an individual may experience inclinations towards self-destructive behavior. Individuals who possess insufficient vital energy in their base chakra often exhibit a heightened vulnerability to the development of hoarding addictions. This signifies their means of attaining control. They experience apprehension regarding their financial matters, encompassing their residential properties and professional pursuits. Those who possess an inadequate level of energy in their root chakra may experience a sense of disorientation. They are likely to perceive a deficiency in their sense of purpose or guidance. They typically face challenges or difficulties when it comes to discovering a meaningful essence in life.

What are the Factors That Contribute to an Imbalance in the Root Chakra?

A disharmony in the root chakra may arise during one's formative years. Individuals who have encountered physical mistreatment or endured from serious illnesses during their childhood are more prone to experiencing inadequacy or imbalance in their root chakra. Children who have been forsaken, detached from their guardians, or whose well-being may have been neglected could encounter challenges related to their survival as they progress into adulthood. As adults, these children will have a tendency to jump from one job to the next or move from house to house. They have a propensity for lacking or encountering challenges with regards to stability. Nevertheless, should individuals effectively restore the vitality of their root chakra, they will greatly enhance their prospects of advancing and achieving a more prosperous existence imbued with harmonious interpersonal connections.

Suggestions for Nurturing and Harmonizing the Root Chakra

In order to attain restoration or restore equilibrium within your root chakra energy, it is imperative to first identify the occurrences in your life that may be eliciting the issue. It is imperative to thoroughly examine these matters in order to determine effective strategies for reversing the situation. Should these concerns remain unresolved, the prospect of progress may prove challenging. Now digging on your past may not exactly be something you are excited to do but know it is a necessary step in healing your root chakra.

The matter does not conclude solely with the restoration of your foundational chakra. It is imperative to consistently engage in efforts to maintain its equilibrium. As you effectively address previous concerns, fresh obstacles will be encountered in your path.

Sustained dedication is necessary in order to harmonize and restore equilibrium to the foundational chakra. Fortunately, there are straightforward measures you can undertake in this regard.

There are a variety of actions that can be taken to reinstate equilibrium in your root chakra. These activities include engaging in culinary pursuits, partaking in physical exercise, strolling outdoors barefoot or vigorously stomping one's feet on the ground, engaging in dance, indulging in a specially prepared meal, playing financial games such as Monopoly, embracing a tree, finding solace in the aesthetic allure of nature, participating in charitable endeavors like volunteering at a soup kitchen or aiding in the construction of homes, engaging in household cleaning or decluttering, practicing meditation, and employing visualization techniques involving the growth of roots extending from one's feet into the earth, among other practices.

Additional suggested activities encompass the execution of both the yoga bridge pose and the crow pose. Consuming foods with high protein content, as well as incorporating red meats and root vegetables into one's diet.

Wear Red

The hue of crimson elicits a favorable influence on this particular energy center. Under such circumstances, the act of donning garments in the color red and adorning oneself with red gemstones may be advantageous. It is recommended that you incorporate red-colored foods into your diet as well. This category encompasses strawberries, tomatoes, and red peppers.

In addition to donning it, it is recommended that you visualize the color radiating vividly at the site of this particular chakra situated at the lower end of your vertebral column. Envision the hue surrounding the foundation of your coccyx. Envision a crimson light descending from the vertebral column, traversing the lower extremities, and ultimately establishing a connection with the ground, thereby anchoring you to the earth.

This is applicable in the case of diminished vitality. In the event of an excessive level of root chakra energy, one may mitigate it by adorning oneself with the color blue.

Listening to C Notes

Music can be beneficial in the endeavor of harmonizing the root chakra, particularly compositions that incorporate the C note. Listen to classical music. Engage in recreational activities during moments of tranquility.

Perform Meditation

Discover a serene and cozy location wherein you may unwind and settle yourself in tranquility without encountering any disruptions. Close your eyes. Imagine the manifestation of energy emanating from the hue of red. To enhance the energy of your root chakra, employ the technique of mentally projecting the color red.

Alternatively, envision the hue of blue in a different context.

Envision the infusion of color as it emanates towards you, manifesting in the shape of a disc enveloping your physical presence, situated at the foundational region of your spinal column. Take a deep inhalation through the nostrils followed by an exhalation through the oral cavity. Engage in this practice while visualizing your breath flowing into the root chakra, manifesting as a vibrant red energetic essence.

Dance for a Workout

Do not allow any feelings of incompetence in dancing or a perceived absence of rhythm deter you from engaging in the activity. It is highly encouraged to synchronize your movements with the rhythm. If dancing is not particularly your preference, an alternative option is to participate in vocalization, as it aids in the purification of the throat chakra. If you sing and dance at the same time then you're hitting two birds with one stone.

Do Yoga

Certain postures can be practiced to purify and harmonize the energy flow of the root chakra. The tree pose is one such example. To execute this position, commence by securely anchoring your left foot onto the mat. The subsequent action entails elevating the right foot. Ensure that your hip is oriented in a forward-facing direction. Please ensure that you position your toes inwardly while shifting your foot to the lateral side of your knee.

Activate your central muscles and proceed to position your right leg into a half lotus. Please raise your arms until they are extended vertically above your head. Please ensure that your elbows maintain a straight position whilst maneuvering your pinky. Relax your neck. Make sure you are grounded firmly to the earth. Maintain the pose for approximately five to eight respiratory cycles prior to transitioning to the opposite side.

Walk Zen Style

It entails more than merely walking, although regular walking can also prove beneficial. Do a mindful walking. Direct your attention to your lower extremity as it becomes disengaged from the surface. Make an effort to establish a connection with the earth with every stride you make. This activity has the potential to alleviate psychological stress while simultaneously purifying the energy center associated with your foundation, known as the root chakra.

Love Your Feet

Another method to attain equilibrium in your root chakra is by attending to the well-being of your feet. Indulge in a professional foot care session. When indulging in self-care, it is crucial to not neglect the well-being of your feet. Value them with the same level of affection that you hold for the entirety of your physical being.

It is widely believed that the base chakra serves as the primary source of energy supply to the remaining chakras. The lack of equilibrium in this particular chakra is bound to adversely affect the well-being of the remaining chakras. As previously stated, the inaugural chakra functions as the bedrock of the chakra system. To put it differently, it is imperative in fostering a harmonious and equitable flow of chakra energy.

Chakras And Science

For a considerable duration, science exhibited an inability or reluctance to investigate the chakras and the practice of chakra healing. While there exists a scarcity of Western scientific evidence substantiating the chakra energy centers, it is evident that the functioning of your body is attributed to the systems or energetic impulses that reside within it. All your actions and thoughts are governed by this intricate system of energy, a fact that has been consistently substantiated by Western scientific research. Merely by observing the electrochemical activity of the brain, one can discern the dominant influence exerted by energy over this crucial organ. Prior to the advent of modern science, the concept of chakras served as a viable means of elucidating the functional processes or fundamental capabilities inherent to the human body. Now, while science may have designated these characteristics with alternative terminology, or may still lack a comprehensive explanation for the functioning of certain physiological aspects, there are undeniable points of convergence between this age-old scientific discipline and the contemporary understanding.

One common point of agreement between science and the concept of chakras is that the human body, along with its surroundings, is comprised of energy. Indeed, the truth of the matter is that the objects in your vicinity are not truly solid entities of reality; rather, they consist merely of a cluster of energetic particles that have temporarily chosen to coalesce. Think about a chair. Though it might give the impression of being robust and stable, fundamentally, it is merely an amalgamation of atoms. Atoms are neither composed of solid matter nor characterized by immobility. Within these atoms, there exist infinitesimal particles in a state of perpetual motion and continual adaptation. Those particles do not possess a solid nature, either. The entities residing within the atomic structure are referred to as subatomic particles, which encompass electrons, neutrons, and protons. The neutrons and protons congregate in the nucleus of the atom, while the electrons orbit in the outer regions. The rapid motion of electrons renders it challenging for scientists to ascertain their precise position from one moment to the next.

Furthermore, aside from its composition of energy, rapidly moving electrons, and densely packed subatomic particles, the fundamental structure of an atom predominantly comprises vacant space. Furthermore, it is approximated that a significant proportion of each atom consists of empty space, amounting to 99.99%. This spatial arrangement facilitates the mobility observed. This information holds veracity not only pertaining to the chair in question, but also encompassing every element within your immediate surroundings, including yourself. Both your physical and mental faculties are subject to perpetual transformation and motion, operating on a level far more intricate than your subjective perception may acknowledge or comprehend. There is not a single entity in existence within this world that does not possess energy.

Science has currently attained the capability to comprehend and substantiate this fact, while religions have long recognized the profound influence of energy in one's existence for countless millennia. Chakras, tai chi, yoga, QiGong, and reiki are all instances of spiritual disciplines centered around the manipulation and harmonization of one's vital energy. The objective of this endeavor is to facilitate the attainment of a state of wellness and equilibrium within your body and being. These ancient belief systems comprehend the interplay between influence and reciprocation: the exchange and flow of energy that occurs as a result of one's actions, including their thoughts. This phenomenon can be attributed to the fact that your brain is in a state of movement and that thoughts play a significant role in constructing your perceived reality.

Scientific inquiry has initiated the elucidation of certain aspects pertaining to the phenomenon of motion and transfer. For instance, even during periods of slumber, one's body remains active in the process of redistributing energy. As per scientific knowledge, this phenomenon primarily occurs via neuronal activity and nerve pathways. In the realms of antiquated sciences and spiritual ideologies, the elucidation of this phenomenon was conveyed by means of the chakras and nadis. Irrespective of one's conscious or subconscious actions, the human body functions as a conduit of continuous energy flow. Some examples of alternative phrasing in a formal tone could be: - These functions encompass the processes of food digestion, cognitive activity, physical locomotion, respiration, and the ability to self-repair. - These activities comprise the mechanisms of nutrient assimilation, mental cognition, bodily mobility, respiratory activity, and self-regeneration. - These actions encompass the capacity to break down food, engage in cognitive processes, execute physical movements, perform respiratory functions, and undergo self-healing.

The neural impulses conveyed by the nervous system propagate from the cranial region to the peripheral regions of the body, and subsequently recirculate from the body to the cranial region. There exist receptors distributed throughout your entire body, enabling you to synchronize your actions with your requirements and desires. Once again, this encompasses both the deliberate and involuntary behaviors performed by your body. When an individual raises their arm, they effectively utilize their neurological system, facilitating the transmission of energy to elevate the mentioned limb. Upon consumption, your body initiates a sequence of vigorous physiological processes aimed at the digestion, assimilation, and subsequent elimination of ingested food. The aforementioned instances illustrate both volitional and non-volitional activities that necessitate energy expenditure and involve the exchange of information between receptors and the brain.

In ancient religious practices, there exist numerous methods to channel this energy effectively, thereby facilitating optimal bodily functionality. Activities such as engaging in various yoga poses, practicing meditation, and adopting deep breathing techniques serve as effective means to facilitate the flow of energy and reinstate a state of harmonious equilibrium within one's life. An alternative approach to alleviate energetic imbalances involves the practice of chakra healing and harmonization, which typically involves employing a diverse array of techniques aimed at facilitating the smooth flow of your life force. Both quantum mechanics as well as conventional scientific principles indicate that directing conscious attention towards one's thoughts has the potential to significantly impact one's overall state of well-being. As an illustration, the application of visualization techniques has demonstrated notable efficacy in enhancing cognitive capabilities and mitigating the decline of cerebral faculties in individuals afflicted by adverse consequences stemming from a stroke. Directing attention towards the chakras and the flow of energy in the nadis is a highly effective approach, which has been practiced for countless centuries and finds validation in contemporary scientific research. This methodology serves to cultivate serenity and enhance overall holistic welfare in one's existence. Although it may bear a different designation, it exhibits remarkable resemblance to each other.

The true manifestation of your energetic essence, consisting of these subtle energetic impulses, is most prominently unveiled within the confines of your heart and brain. The human brain serves as an excellent reservoir for observing the profound influence of energy within the body. Within the confines of your cerebral cortex, a staggering number of over one hundred billion neural pathways exist, facilitating the transmission of electrical impulses responsible for various cognitive processes. These impulses correspond to the flow of charged ions within your body, regulating cardiovascular function and facilitating muscular contractions. They represent essential biological pathways necessary for optimal physiological functioning. Examining the electrical activity of the brain presents a valuable means of comprehending the energetic composition of the human body.

Apart from the inherent energy within your being, there is also a surrounding energy that envelops your physical form. It can be challenging to grasp the presence of an electromagnetic field enveloping your body, despite perceiving the physical boundaries of your skin and the opposing solidity of your bones. This exhibits a particular frequency. This may initially appear to be unconventional and archaic until one comprehends that scientists employ this knowledge in the quantification of such frequencies using sophisticated instruments such as MRI or ECG machines. An alteration in the energy state within a specific vicinity indicates an inherent imbalance, which can be visually discerned through the generated images produced by these apparatus.

Psychology represents a contemporary scientific domain dedicated to investigating the human mind, as well as comprehending the underlying causes behind our cognitive processes and behavioral patterns. As indicated by the findings of Psychology Today, each individual represents a corporeal manifestation of an energetic realm. The chakras elucidate the existence of focal points within the body, serving as conduits for the flow of this energy. These movements regulate and influence various aspects of your physiology, including emotions, organ functioning, and immune responses, among other factors. In a state of harmonious alignment, one finds oneself spiritually, physically, emotionally, and mentally balanced, allowing for the smooth flow of all aspects of being. Henceforth, the utmost significance lies within the fundamental role that your chakras play in nurturing your holistic welfare.

Conversely, should there be an obstruction in your energy flow, it can result in the manifestation of illness. This phenomenon is evident in scientific evaluations, such as CT scans or MRIs. A tumor presents itself as a darkened region within an otherwise dynamic and fluidic system. The obstructed flow of energy in that particular location is adversely affecting your well-being. On other occasions, it becomes evident in one's cognitive capacity. An obstruction in the flow of energy can lead to the occurrence of psychological disorders such as anxiety, depression, or other related conditions. Engaging in techniques aimed at purifying and mobilizing one's energy can be an incredibly potent instrument. According to a recent study, participants who experienced a stroke exhibited noteworthy enhancements in cerebral health through the practice of mental imagery, specifically visualizing lifting a limb that had been rendered paralyzed as a result of the stroke. The stroke damaged a part of their brain that sends the energetic information to that limb to move but visualizing it moving helped strengthen the brain tissue around that damaged area so the deterioration did not spread. This serves as a singular contemporary scientific illustration, demonstrating how an age-old practice of manipulating energy through cognitive processes can lead to notable enhancements in one's physical state of health.

It is widely recognized that one's psychological well-being has a significant influence on their physical well-being. This phenomenon is most evident in the association between stress and one's overall well-being.

Stress is a psychological and cognitive condition; however, excessive presence of stress triggers a series of physiological maladies in conjunction. As per the findings of the National Institute of Health, stress can be characterized as a state of imbalance within one's life. This disparity, whether actual or perceived, prompts the body to seek out and reinstate equilibrium. These scenarios induce the secretion of highly potent stress-releasing hormones, triggering a state of heightened anxiety and stimulation. According to present-day scientific research, stress is identified as a significant contributing factor to various ailments, including cancer and mental disorders. Every year, stress incurs millions of dollars in medical expenditures. This topic is a perpetual subject of debate in contemporary science, and it is widely acknowledged by the majority of medical professionals and researchers that the mitigation of stress plays a crucial role in bolstering one's holistic well-being.

Furthermore, present-day scientific and medical communities are increasingly comprehending and advocating for the holistic well-being of individuals, encompassing both mental and physical aspects. Evidence has increasingly indicated that an individual's psychological well-being is of equal, if not greater, significance than their physical condition in reestablishing equilibrium within their overall well-being. Comprehensive care encompasses not only the physical aspects but also the mental and spiritual dimensions. As per the findings presented by the National Institute of Health, the majority of literature pertaining to the spiritual or mental healing of individuals tends to possess a predominantly spiritual essence. Consequently, this subject matter remains unfamiliar to a large number of medical professionals. However, it is imperative for Western medicine to embark upon the establishment of a more all-encompassing framework capable of addressing the physical and metaphysical aspects of an individual's being. This implies that an ongoing exploration of the relationship between the energetics of the mind, spirit, and the physical body is essential for Western scientific advancements in patient care.

Nearly a century ago, within the Western region, Sir William Osler recorded an instance in which a patient experienced an asthma exacerbation upon exposure to the scent of an artificial rose. This presented an intriguing query that was beyond the grasp of contemporary scientific understanding. There existed no plausible physiological cause for this occurrence. In the year 1975, Dr. Robert Adler provided a rationale that postulates an individual's thoughts as having the ability to influence their immune system. Sir William Osler's curiosity regarding the mechanisms behind mammals' ability to regulate immune responses led him to seek an explanation from Dr. Adler, who ultimately provided a comprehensive elucidation. Through his experiments, Dr. Adler conclusively demonstrated the profound impact of an individual's emotions and thoughts on their physiological well-being, including the remarkable influence on their bodily functions and immune response.

Prior to these discoveries, Western science held the belief that each bodily system functioned autonomously from one another. According to the premise of our contemporary scientific knowledge, it has been posited that the immune system remains unaffected by one's emotional or mental condition. Dr. Adler has provided evidence that contradicts this assertion. His research findings revealed a significant correlation between the interplay of all bodily systems, ultimately influencing each component to achieve equilibrium or homeostasis. Furthermore, it was his research results that initially elucidated the detrimental effects of stress on one's physical welfare.

There is a growing acknowledgement among conventional, Western medical practitioners that one's psychological well-being significantly influences their physical health, a concept that has long been recognized in Eastern traditions spanning millenniums. The wisdom of antiquity recognized that vitality emanates from energy, and any disturbance or disharmony in this vital force can profoundly affect one's physical well-being. Unhindered circulation of energy is imperative, and one can accomplish this objective by undertaking specific measures to attain equilibrium. One can employ techniques such as meditation, visualization, consumption of specific foods, engagement in particular physical activities, and more. To facilitate the circulation of this life force, commonly referred to as vital energy, throughout your physique, and establish a state of equilibrium. By maintaining the clarity and unobstructed flow of these energy hubs or channels, akin to ensuring the absence of plaque within your arteries to facilitate unhindered blood circulation, you can cultivate a state of improved health and harmony in your life. Regrettably, a significant number of Western cultures do not prioritize this comprehensive approach. Consequently, this leads to energy centers becoming dormant, inactive, or obstructed. Consequently, this engenders a disturbance in the equilibrium of energy, thereby resulting in ailments and disharmony.

The Seven Chakras

As covered in the preceding chapter, it is imperative to take into account the existence of seven fundamental chakras. While there exists a belief held by a faction positing that the count may extend to 114, the prevailing majority tends to direct their attention solely towards these fundamental seven. Every chakra exercises jurisdiction over a distinct range of sensations, sentiments, bodily functions, and conduct. Additionally, they possess distinct hues and are positioned at the lowermost part. In this chapter, we shall delve further into the understanding of each of the seven chakras. We shall commence with the chakra located at the base of your spinal column, commonly referred to as the "root chakra", proceeding subsequently to ascend towards the chakra situated at the apex of your spinal column, known as the "crown chakra". This sequence encompasses a progression spanning from the initial to the subsequent seventh chakra. Throughout the process, you will acquire comprehensive knowledge regarding each subject matter.

The Root Chakra

The primary chakra among the seven is the Root Chakra. This vibrant crimson chakra is positioned at the foundational region of your spinal column, situated between the lower extremities of your body. In certain literary or educational sources, this particular chakra is linked to an Earthy brown hue, as opposed to a red shade.

The Root Chakra holds the responsibility for bestowing a profound sense of grounding and stability in one's life, along with cultivating a deep-rooted feeling of security. A prevalent indication of the misalignment of this chakra is a sensation of apprehension. This symptom can be manifested regardless of whether this chakra is hypoactive or hyperactive. In the event that you are currently afflicted with a depleted Root Chakra, it is highly probable that you will also encounter emotions surrounding a perceived lack of security or trepidation in various aspects of your existence. In the event of its excessive activation, you may experience a sense of being entrenched in old habits or difficulties in embracing transition or change in your personal life. Nevertheless, the most effective approach to attaining equilibrium in this chakra entails engaging in meditation and honing grounding techniques. By doing so, you will contribute to the mitigation of numerous associated afflictions.

This chakra is closely linked to vital organs including the kidneys, reproductive glands and organs, as well as the spinal column. If you encounter any challenges such as renal infections, discomfort, reproductive impairments or disruptions in reproductive hormones, or spinal discomfort, it is possible that the malalignment of your Root Chakra is the underlying cause. It is highly probable that you can reinstate equilibrium to your chakra and encounter decreased stress within any of these systems.

The Sacral Chakra

The Sacral Chakra is identified as the second energy center amongst the seven chakras. This particular chakra can be found positioned superior to the pelvis, residing betwixt the hip regions. This chakra exhibits a vibrational affinity with the hue of orange.

The Sacral Chakra governs one's fervor, sexual energy, and artistic expression. When one encounters a deficiency in the function of their Sacral Chakra, they may encounter difficulties in fostering creativity, experience a sense of indifference or inflexibility, or perceive a barrier to cultivating emotional intimacy. In instances where this chakra is excessively inactive, one may encounter a deficiency in both physical and emotional intimacy. In an alternative scenario, should the aforementioned chakra exhibit excessive activity, an individual may experience an intensified sense of sexuality, to the extent that they might be perceived as displaying tendencies akin to that of someone grappling with sexual addiction. Additionally, you might discover that you are prone to developing emotional attachments quite readily. In any case, it is imperative that you allocate the necessary time to restore equilibrium to your Sacral Chakra. One may accomplish this by practicing meditation, cultivating mindfulness, and employing some of the natural techniques elaborated upon subsequently in this publication.

This particular chakra exhibits a direct correlation with bodily organs, namely the gallbladder, adrenal glands, immune system, excretory organs, metabolic processes, and the spleen. When encountering imbalances in any of these chakras, it is imperative to devote sufficient time towards restoring equilibrium to your Sacral Chakra. By doing so, it is probable that you will substantially alleviate a significant portion of your adverse side effects and symptoms.

The Chakra located in the region of the solar plexus

The third chakra, known as the Solar Plexus Chakra, exhibits a placement that may appear evident once more. It is situated in the region of the solar plexus, positioned slightly above the umbilicus. This chakra of a radiant golden hue possesses significant strength and is renowned for its profound connection to various aspects of our existence.

The Solar Plexus Chakra assumes responsibility for instilling emotions of self-assurance, determination, individual authority, and vigor. When one experiences any sort of disrupted energy flow within the chakra system, it becomes challenging to effectively cope with the associated emotional consequences. When the Solar Plexus Chakra is not functioning optimally, one may experience a sense of powerlessness, timidity, or lack of self-assurance. If individuals are experiencing diminished self-esteem, it is frequently linked to this specific chakra, as well. It is possible that you may also experience a dearth of direction or purpose in your life. In the event of an excessive activation of this particular chakra, an individual may possibly exhibit tendencies towards aggression or dominance, accompanied by an inclination to assume authoritative control in various circumstances. Neither is a goal that you should aspire to attain. Restoring equilibrium to this chakra will facilitate a heightened sense of self-assurance and empowerment without the need to adopt an overbearing disposition.

The physiological systems associated with the Solar Plexus Chakra encompass the cervical spine, hepatic structure, gastrointestinal tract, pancreatic function, and metabolic activities. In the event of an imbalance in this chakra, individuals may encounter physical discomfort or health issues within any of the aforementioned systems. When the chakra is aligned and harmonized, it is highly probable that each individual chakra will exhibit enhanced functionality, ultimately contributing to an overall improvement in your holistic well-being.

Chakra Mudras

The term "Mudra" originates from the Sanskrit language. Its meaning is "seal". A Mudra is established through the act of positioning or interlacing the hands and fingers in various configurations to yield specific outcomes. Mudra, as per the ancient vedic literature, has been articulated as "gestures designed to invoke favor from the celestial beings and deities, while also facilitating the dissipation of negative impressions, and fulfilling one's inner yearnings." Mudras enable us to transcend the realm of mundane consciousness and ascend to a sublime level of elevated consciousness, ultimately reaching a state of utmost spiritual enlightenment.

Mudras are classified into three distinct categories.

1. The utilization of mudras within the practices of meditation and yoga. Exterior mudras can be observed in the manifestation of corporeal poses such as yoga asanas. Conversely, inner mudras are associated with practices of meditation and the enhancement of concentration.

2. Within the depths of our being lie intrinsic seals or mudras, manifested through the distinctive patterns etched upon our foreheads, the countenance that adorns our visage, the harmonious arrangement and equilibrium inherent in our physical structure, and the intricate lines delicately traced upon our soles and palms. The study of discerning a person's character by analyzing their body configurations is referred to as Sumudraka Shastra.

3. Manual gestures employed to activate specific energies. The fingers present

herein are associated with various forms of energy. When combining them in specific manners, they yield nuanced outcomes. The deliberate placement of hands facilitates the unobstructed circulation of energy. They possess the ability to restore equilibrium to the seven chakras within the body.

Mudras have the potential to facilitate spiritual progress. Mudras have the capacity to convey countless potentials and profound enigmas that exist independent of our corporeal existence. You can achieve remarkable outcomes through the practice of these mudras. In addition, they have the potential to enhance your overall well-being.

Hand gestures for the Seven Chakras

Performing the hand gesture for activating the Muladhara Chakra involves bringing the tips of the index finger and thumb into contact. Focus on the spot between the anus and genitals. Chant the LAM sound.

To activate the Svadhisthana Chakra, it is advised to position your hands on your lap, with the palms facing upwards and placed gently on top of one another. Ensure that the left hand remains positioned below, while bringing the palms of your hands into contact with the posterior side of your fingers on the right hand. It is advisable that the tips of your thumbs make light contact with each other. Direct your attention to the chakra situated within the sacral region, specifically located in the lower back area. Continue to vocalize the VAM sound.

Mudra for Manipura Chakra – Position your hands anteriorly to the abdominal region, slightly beneath the solar plexus.

Enable your digits to combine with the apex. They should point away. Cross your thumbs. It is advised to ensure that your fingers remain in a straight position. Direct your attention to the chakra positioned along your spinal column, just slightly superior to your navel. Chant the RAM sound.

Mudra for Anahata Chakra – It is recommended to assume a seated position with crossed legs. Permit the tips of your thumb and index finger to make contact with one another. Ensure that the left hand remains positioned atop the left knee. The placement of the right hand should be positioned anteriorly to the lower aspect of the sternum, slightly anterior to the solar plexus. Direct your attention towards the chakra situated at the level of your spinal cord. Chant the YAM sound.

Perform the gesture for activating the Vishuddha Chakra by interlocking the fingers of the hands together, excluding the thumbs. It is advisable for your thumbs to make contact with the uppermost part. Kindly elevate your fingers gently. Focus on your chakra at the throat's base. Chant the HAM sound.

Gesture for Ajna Chakra - Position your hands in front of the lower part of the chest. Ensure that your middle fingers maintain a straight alignment. They ought to make contact with the highest point, and must be oriented in a forward direction. The remaining digits must undergo flexion. It is necessary for them to make contact with the two upper phalanges. Ensure that the thumbs are directed inwardly as you make contact with the uppermost parts. Direct your attention to the chakra situated slightly above the region between your eyebrows. Recite the sacred syllable AUM or OM.

Perform the hand gesture corresponding to the Sahasrara Chakra by positioning your hands before the abdominal region. Adopt a posture where your ring fingers are oriented upwards. They ought to make contact with their respective peaks. Interlace the remaining fingers, ensuring that your left thumb is positioned below the right thumb. Direct your attention to the chakra located at the apex of your head. Chant the NG sound.

Chakra Energy Flow Maintenance

The activities you engage in on a daily basis - the individuals you encounter, the ideas you contemplate, and the obstacles you encounter - will all have an impact on the equilibrium of your chakras. There is an exchange of energy, which may occasionally result in its concentration within certain areas, necessitating the need for equilibrium. A system that is not in equilibrium will exhibit discernible consequences, including the development of specific cravings or aversions towards certain foods, scents, and colors.

And when it comes to achieving balance, the optimal approach lies in finding the solution that strikes just the right amount, avoiding both excessive and insufficient measures. An adequately harmonized system will engender a feeling of creativity, vitality, and assurance in the belief that your decisions are optimally suited to your needs. Conversely, the process of verifying your balance is effortless and can be elucidated as follows.

Similar to any physical activity, it is possible to experience an imbalance, and taking proactive steps to address this issue can help avert any subsequent complications. When a chakra becomes imbalanced, another aspect will accordingly adjust, resulting in a heightened sensation of frustration within various domains. This serves as a valuable cautionary reminder for the need to restore equilibrium within oneself.

Balancing

This exercise is highly effective in restoring equilibrium to each individual chakra. In a manner akin to exercise two, this exercise shall address every individual chakra, affording you the opportunity to identify any imbalances necessitating additional purification and recuperation. Alternatively, it may serve to rectify any imbalances you may encounter throughout the day, thereby sustaining your equilibrium.

Upon establishing a stable connection with the earth, envision yourself being infused with the luminosity of every individual chakra. One should experience a sensation of tingling or perceive a subtle shift in perception with the presence of each distinct color. After this occurrence, proceed to advance to the subsequent hue while making mental observations regarding the duration required for the energy movement to be perceived. Upon reaching the crown chakra, it is advisable to visualize oneself enveloped within a sphere of luminous white radiance, incorporating a lacing of violet hues to enhance the experience. Subsequently, one may assess if any discernible alterations in the lower energetic centers are perceivable. Reconnect with your surroundings, returning to a state of mindful awareness.

In certain instances, this practice alone may suffice to restore equilibrium to your chakras. However, it is often the case that this will underscore areas that require increased focus and attention. Facilitating the restoration of their energy centers necessitates a thorough purification and therapeutic treatment of each individual one.

By engaging in this daily routine, you will develop an enhanced sense of the energy dynamics within your body, enabling you to rectify any minor disharmonies that might arise. Do not permit this to evolve into an obligation: having an awareness of the movement of energy necessitates only a brief period of time and enhances the ease and effectiveness of decision-making.

It is essential to ensure that you realign yourself with the root chakra, ensuring that the energetic flow is unobstructed. While this sensation may elicit a pleasant feeling, an extended duration of such practice can severely disrupt the proper equilibrium of your chakra system. Excessive flow of energy within the chakras can impede the harmonious circulation of energies emanating from other chakras, while also drawing both favorable and unfavorable energy to the affected chakra. Merely savoring the uninhibited movement of energy and subsequently reintegrating it to your accustomed state of awareness shall maintain equilibrium within your system, thereby averting potential misinterpretations concerning your demeanor.

Significant disparities, particularly an energy influx that contradicts the harmonious flow of the other chakras, are indicative of an issue. This will impede the efficient transmission of energy, and give rise to nuanced complications in your daily experiences. Fortunately, there are methods available to restore and purify this condition, and notably, some of them are accessible at no cost.

Chapter 2: The Primary energy centers within the human body

As previously mentioned, it has been stipulated that there exist seven vital chakras within the human body. This chapter offers a comprehensive account of the chakras, encompassing an extensive range of knowledge pertaining to their inherent nature as well as the corresponding chromatic associations.

The Root Chakra

This represents the primary energy center, also known as the root chakra, situated at the lowermost point of your vertebral column. This particular chakra holds utmost significance and necessitates continuous balance. This energy center facilitates the establishment of interpersonal connections encompassing one's family, community, and cultural framework. This particular energy center is consistently linked with sentiments of gratification, distress, sexual impulses, and primal survival instincts, frequently identified with the hue red.

The Sacral Chakra

The second chakra in the sequence is the sacral chakra, which is correlated with the hue of orange. The sacral chakra is situated below the navel and is intricately connected to one's creative aptitude and instinctual nature. If one discovers oneself prepared for embarking on an expedition, it can be confidently inferred that the equilibrium of the sacral chakra has been attained. This is associated with your inclination toward playfulness, emotions, and your inner child as well.

The Solar Plexus
The solar plexus corresponds to the third chakra, which is consistently connected to the color yellow. This particular energy center originates from the region of the abdomen and extends towards the chest area. It is intrinsically connected to one's self-esteem, perception of personal value, response to critique, and uniqueness as an individual.

The Heart Chakra

The heart chakra, referred to as the fourth chakra, is situated in the center of the chest. This particular chakra is affiliated with the hues of pink and green and is interconnected with one's self-assurance, inspiration, and sense of self-assurance. Furthermore, it is correlated with your affection towards individuals.

The Throat Chakra
This marks the fifth chakra and is situated precisely at the lower point of your throat. This particular chakra holds significance as it is intricately connected to one's capacity for sound decision-making and aptitude for assuming authority when required. You will discover a profound sense of creativity bestowed upon you when the equilibrium of this chakra is established. This chakra is further associated with various forms of energies, with particular emphasis placed on the

significance of expressing truthful information. The hue linked to this chakra is blue.

The Brow Chakra

The sixth chakra, otherwise known as the brow chakra, frequently denotes the third eye chakra and pertains to the aspect of your attention. The nomenclature assigned to this chakra stems from its specific location situated precisely betwixt the eyebrows upon the expanse of one's forehead. This chakra is closely associated with attributes such as sagacity, intellect, comprehension, and internal sight. The chakra is commonly linked with the hue of indigo.

The Crown Chakra

The ultimate chakra, known as the crown chakra, is situated in the highest region of the head. This can be likened to the regal headpiece worn by a monarch.

This particular chakra is correlated with the hues of violet and pristine white. This particular chakra exhibits a perpetual connection with a transcendent force, facilitating an existence guided by the present moment and enabling an unwavering commitment towards the pursuit of one's most cherished aspirations.

Reestablishing Balance In The Third Eye Chakra

The lot's sixth chakra is denoted by the term 'third eye' chakra, which is alternatively known as the 'brow' chakra and the 'ajna' chakra in Sanskrit. The hue of this object can be described as indigo, and it is commonly linked to the concept of 'extra-sensory perception'. Its representation is depicted in the symbol presented hereafter.

What are the Functions and Purposes of the Third Eye Chakra?

The third eye chakra is situated at the midpoint between the eyebrows, playing a significant role in guiding intuitive actions, providing direction in life, and overseeing the functioning of the pituitary gland, lower cerebral region, and cranium. It serves to govern one's capacity to cultivate precise intuition, anticipate events, perceive the broader perspective in one's existence, ascertain one's purpose and aspirations, and maintain emotional equilibrium.

What are the effects of an open and blocked sixth chakra?

In the event that the sixth chakra is unobstructed, one comprehends their life's vision and purpose effortlessly, demonstrating proficiency in establishing and actively pursuing objectives until their fruition. Your innate capacity for intuition is also enhanced, enabling you to anticipate future events. Additionally, your gastrointestinal system, pituitary gland, and cerebral function operate at an optimal level.

In contrast, if the ajna chakra is obstructed, one may encounter challenges in accessing their intuitive faculties and placing confidence in their internal guidance. Additionally, you encounter difficulties in acquiring novel knowledge and acquiring new skills, as well as retrieving information in a timely manner. Furthermore, you exhibit challenges in comprehending and pursuing your life's purpose and aspirations, along with a notable deficiency in your intuitive faculties. In addition, you experience symptoms of paranoia, indecisiveness, headaches, eye discomfort, sinus problems, back pain, leg aches, and a sense of aimlessness. Fortunately, we possess the appropriate strategies to alleviate these issues.

What are the Methods for Reestablishing Equilibrium in Your Third Eye Chakra?

"Engage in the following principles to facilitate unobstructed movement of energy within your sixth chakra:

Crystal Healing

Purple Fluorite, Black Obsidian, and Amethyst possess remarkable properties that facilitate the restoration and balancing of the third eye chakra. These exquisite gemstones effectively enhance intuitive abilities, dissolve cognitive confusion, and enable effortless foresight. One may choose to don the gemstones in the form of a pendant or bracelet, alternatively, one could opt to grasp them for a duration of 10 minutes each day.

Meditative Practice

Kindly shut your eyes, assume a composed seated position, and engage in the act of taking ten deliberate, unhurried breaths. Bring your attention to your third eye chakra and imagine an indigo colored light in between your eyebrows. Imagine it gradually intensifying its radiance and spreading throughout your entire being. Devote 10 to 20 minutes to engaging in this exercise, followed by profound contemplation of your prominent concerns, free from any form of bias and with an objective mindset. Consistently engage in this activity on a daily basis and in due course, you will develop the aptitude to perceive matters with clarity and consequently make more informed decisions.

Eat Healthy

Furthermore, it is recommended to include in your diet foods such as dark chocolate, rich sources of omega-3 fatty acids like salmon and walnuts, nutrient-dense items like chia seeds and eggs, as well as purple hued foods such as purple cabbage, eggplant, and blackberries. These dietary choices are believed to promote the harmonious and uninterrupted flow of energy within the sixth chakra.

Affirmations

Additionally, make it a regular practice to recite the following affirmations with the intention of activating your ajna chakra.

I possess strong intuitive capabilities and a notable aptitude for accurate foresight.

I possess a high level of competency in decision-making, consistently demonstrating aptitude and finesse in this realm.

I have adeptly tapped into my intuitions, enabling me to discern a definitive purpose in my existence.

I am currently pursuing my life's purpose and aligning my actions with my long-term objectives.

Now that you have acquired the knowledge pertaining to the harmonization of all six chakras, let us proceed to the concluding section and acquire the skills necessary to stabilize them.

Comprehending The Fundamentals Of Your Energetic Chakras

Could you please provide a precise explanation of the concept of a chakra? Although the term may appear somewhat uncertain, the concept of chakras can be delineated, albeit with minor variations in definition depending on the perspective and situational context of the individual providing it. The notion of the chakra and numerous exercises linked to it originate from India. These traditions have endured for millennia. Indeed, the term "chakra" has derived its origins from the archaic Sanskrit language, renowned as one of the most ancient languages to have existed throughout human history. The term "chakra" possesses a connotation of "wheel" in its translation, and this association becomes evident when one contemplates the functioning of the chakras within the confines of the human body.

The chakras can be described as an intricate network of wheels within the human body, continually rotating and facilitating the unobstructed movement of energy. Alternatively, one can characterize them as a network of energy channels. These pathways facilitate the transmission of energy throughout the body, distributing it internally at distinct intervals and contributing to the operation of diverse biological and spiritual systems within. Similar to the physiological channels found in the human body, namely veins, arteries, and intestines, the chakras can experience obstructions or impediments that hinder the smooth circulation of energy within the body. As a consequence, these blockages can give rise to a range of issues that manifest at the mental, physical, or spiritual level.

Each chakra can be categorized into two distinct groups: the physical chakra and the spiritual chakra. The corporeal chakras furnish energies to fulfill your physical needs and desires, whereas the ethereal ones supply energies for the nourishment of your soul. The fourth chakra serves as the intermediary between these two realms, which, although distinct, are mutually interconnected, and it cannot be categorized as either one.

For the purposes of this book, we will allow that there are seven chakras in the body (some people hold the belief that there are four, although seven is the most commonly accepted number). They are situated in proximity to various nerve centers and vital organs within the human body along the spinal column, and each individual chakra plays a crucial role in distinct physiological and psychological processes. Every physiological system within our bodies corresponds to a specific chakra, which is situated in close proximity to the nerves and vital organs associated with that particular system. This correlation underscores the utmost significance of maintaining optimal physical well-being for our chakras. Enabling unimpeded energy flow within the chakras and averting obstructions or excessive stimulation thereof has a direct impact on one's physical well-being.

If a particular chakra fails to generate or facilitate the unhindered movement of energy, it can be said that the chakra is obstructed. If the level of energy production or intake exceeds an optimal threshold, it can be classified as excessively active. Both conditions can have severe adverse effects on your well-being.

The initial chakra is referred to as the root chakra, with its Sanskrit counterpart being Muladhara. The fundamental chakra represents the region of the pelvic floor, which holds substantial energetic significance within the body. Additionally, it encompasses the lower three vertebrae of the spine, the spinal base, and the anus. Muladhara comprises the amalgamation of the Sanskrit term Mula, denoting the concept of 'root', and the term adhara, signifying 'support'. This particular chakra bears a fitting designation, as it serves as the foundation, fostering a connection between individuals and the terrestrial realm, as well as the realm of intrinsic elements. In its capacity as the primary chakra, it fulfills a vital function in ensuring security and stability throughout your chakra system, as well as within your psyche and physical being. The equilibrium of the system cannot be attained unless there is an unobstructed circulation of energy within the root chakra. Given its critical role as the foundation of the chakra system, maintaining good health in this particular chakra is of utmost importance.

This particular chakra assumes a vital function in providing a foundation for our physical and mental well-being. It pertains to our inherent cognitive perception and olfaction, our primal anxieties, and our innate need for reassurance within the cosmic expanse. It solidifies our connection to the earth, anchoring us in our earthly existence and in the realm of physical reality.

The root chakra represents the realm of safety, safeguarding, and the fulfillment of fundamental needs. This particular chakra establishes a deep connection with us during our formative years, which is advantageous since it helps us retain and understand our feelings of interconnectedness. This knowledge aids us in recapturing those sensations that might fade away as we mature into adulthood.

In Hindu traditional representations, the lotus flower serves as the symbolic manifestation of the root chakra. The floral structure exhibits a quadrilateral arrangement of petals, which are colored in a vibrant shade of red. The lotus flower embodies our inherent essence and the interconnectedness with our environment, whereas the crimson hue represents the profound awakening of our consciousness, both spiritually and physically, essential for harmonizing with the chakra system and attaining wholesome well-being.

The second chakra is referred to as Svadhisthana, also commonly known as the sacral chakra. Svadhisthana, derived from the Sanskrit language, signifies 'the abode of the self'—a commonly held interpretation referring to the dwelling place of consciousness. The area associated with the sacral chakra encompasses the reproductive organs. The hypogastric plexuses can also be found within this particular anatomical region. The sacral chakra emanates from a point located approximately three inches beneath the navel. This chakra pertains to the domains of artistic expression, sexual longing, and bliss, while additionally functioning as an intensely emotive energy center. Consequently, this implies that it holds immense significance as a chakra for humans, capable of bestowing boundless contentment. Nonetheless, the repercussions of its imbalance are remarkably perilous, thereby emphasizing the heightened importance of diligently preserving the well-being of this particular chakra.

The sacral chakra is the energy center that governs the harmonization of our emotions and well-being in the context of our internal, familial, and sexual connections. It governs our capacity to cultivate fulfilling connections and likewise extends to our professional trajectories.

In addition, it serves as the primary energy center associated with our corporeal faculties, encompassing the faculties of tactile perception, auditory discernment, visual reception, and gustatory sensation, faculties that have the capacity to bestow both gratification and suffering upon us. The sacral chakra can be described as imbued with the essence of water, which resonates with the fluidity encompassing our spiritual, mental, and emotional aspects. We have the ability to be artistic, problem-solve and create new systems when this chakra is balanced.

The sacral chakra attains its highest state of openness and well-being during childhood, a time characterized by our greatest degree of receptiveness and spontaneity. The experience of unrestricted play, along with a profound sense of liberation and joy, tends to be more readily attainable during our early years. Nevertheless, in numerous instances, upon the onset of adolescence, we are confronted with the surge of awareness pertaining to sexuality and the subsequent sense of shame, resulting in either an excessive stimulation or impairment of this particular chakra.

The representation of the sacral chakra comes in the form of the lotus flower accompanied by the crescent moon symbol. The flower is orange for emotional stability, the moon a reflection of our emotional, spiritual and physical cycles as human beings.

The Manipura chakra, also known as the warrior chakra, represents the third and last physical energy center. This particular energy center is identified by various designations, such as the solar plexus chakra, albeit for the context presented in this book, the term Warrior is deemed the most precise and appropriate. This chakra is positioned within the midsection of the human body, specifically around the navel region. It serves as the nexus of fortitude, governing the force that resides within, as well as one's perception of personal value and confidence.

A well-balanced warrior chakra bestows upon you the strength of your inner warrior, enabling you to accomplish your objectives and incorporate wholesome lifestyle habits. The warrior chakra centers its focus solely on you. Your strength of determination, the faculty of awareness, and ability to transform both your own being and the surrounding circumstances.

The chakra is profoundly affected by individual determination and diligence. When an individual possesses a comprehensive and encompassing understanding of their self-identity, this particular energy center will manifest in a state of robust health and overall equilibrium. The capacity to persevere and the capacity to relinquish are inherent aspects of one's ego, and both shall function optimally in individuals possessing a robust energetic balance within the warrior chakra.

The warrior chakra exerts its resonance throughout the course of our existence, particularly as we navigate significant junctures and transitions, such as the transition from adolescence to adulthood. It is particularly triggered during periods of adversity. The emblematic symbol of the warrior chakra manifests as a vibrant yellow lotus blossom, adorned gracefully with ten delicately arranged petals. The hue of yellow symbolizes the chakra associated with warriors, signifying their attribute of fire.

The Anahata chakra, otherwise known as the heart chakra, constitutes the fourth energy center in the body. Anahata is a term derived from the Sanskrit language, signifying the concept of being unharmed. The heart chakra pertains to the cardiac region, encompassing the mammary glands and pulmonary system, comprising a vital organ that derives its namesake. The heart chakra one of the most important of your chakras, because it lies neither in the realm of the chakras of physical matter nor in the chakras of spiritual matter but in a place directly in between the two.

The facilitation of energy towards your cardiac chakra aids in the management of distress, sorrow, bereavement, and the process of embracing circumstances. Despite experiencing emotions that may be classified as negative, these feelings are inherent to our human nature and form an integral part of our existence. Effective alignment of energy towards the heart chakra enables one to effectively manage and process such sentiments in a constructive manner, rather than being overwhelmed by their weight. A heart chakra that is receptive and unobstructed will facilitate the exploration of latent yearnings and aspirations, enabling significant determinations to be made.

As the locus of the heart's vital energies, wherein the essence of love materializes, this chakra profoundly influences one's emotional well-being and interpersonal connections. An optimally functioning heart chakra promotes positive interpersonal connections and fosters empathy towards others. You possess a deep sense of empathy and foster meaningful connections with both individuals and the environment. One is capable of perceiving the aesthetic appeal of various objects and experiences, as well as cultivating the ability to understand and share the feelings of others. The heart chakra will remain active throughout the entirety of one's lifespan, encompassing the stages from infancy to the time of death.

The heart chakra holds immense significance as it serves as a conduit linking the tangible and materialistic aspects contained within the lower three chakras, which pertain to physical cravings and requirements, with the ethereal and divine elements present in the upper three chakras, which encompass spiritual essentials and elevated awareness. The heart chakra serves as a central point that, in a state of optimal well-being, seamlessly connects the two realms, enabling the attainment of both spiritual and physical objectives. Ultimately, these objectives and the corresponding chakras are deeply intertwined, such that any impact on one yields repercussions throughout the entire system.

The heart chakra is represented by a hexagram enclosed within the green lotus. This symbolizes the ethereal nature of air, functioning as a mediator between the corporeal and the transcendent. The star symbolizes the interconnectedness facilitated by the heart chakra.

The fifth chakra is identified as the Vishuddha chakra, commonly referred to as the chakra associated with the concept of truth. It is alternatively referred to as the laryngeal chakra. The term "Vishuddha" originates from the Sanskrit language, where it conveys the meaning of "pure." This particular chakra can be found in the vicinity of the throat area, signifying its interconnectedness with the functions of the mouth, speech, and the thyroid gland. The throat chakra governs the articulation of our thoughts and feelings, encompassing both our aspirations and our capacity to communicate them effectively.

The throat chakra is focused on the manifestation of artistic ingenuity and the emission of an authentic and elevated persona into the surrounding environment. It revolves around profound insights into one's own being, encompassing both the physical and spiritual aspects, and empowers one to articulate them. Additionally, it provides you with the means to articulate your desires, afflictions, and other emotions experienced throughout the course of your lifetime.

The genuine essence of your purpose resides within the throat chakra. The proper alignment of this chakra holds significant importance as it lies directly above the heart chakra, thereby exerting influence on its functionality. It is capable of either elevating or reducing the effectiveness of the heart chakra, depending on the dynamic flow of energy.

The throat chakra facilitates a connection with the metaphysical realm of spirituality. The ethereal domain pertains to intangible faculties such as intuition and faith.

The blue lotus flower serves as the symbolic embodiment of the throat chakra. This chakra is devoid of any terrestrial attribute, being of a spiritual nature. However, the color blue in this instance symbolizes the utmost clarity in sound and sagacity, as well as the profound self-awareness emanating from this particular chakra.

What is Aromatherapy?

"Aromatherapy is a compassionate and tactile therapeutic approach that aims to promote relaxation, enhance vitality, alleviate the impact of stress, and rectify inner equilibrium in the realms of mind, body, and spirit." - Robert Tisserand

Aromatherapy is a therapeutic method that employs the use of botanical oils, botanical extracts, and botanical essences to promote relaxation and alleviate the physical, mental, and psychosomatic discomforts that individuals may experience. Aromatherapy is a form of complementary and alternative medicine that is experiencing an increase in prominence within contemporary society. This therapy entails both physiological and psychological repercussions for the human body. The concept of aromatherapy is not novel and has been employed since ancient eras.

The modality by which aromatherapy exerts its effects is straightforward. Upon inhalation of the specific aroma, the process of stimulating the hypothalamus within the cerebral region commences promptly. The hypothalamus serves as the primary organ responsible for effectively regulating important bodily functions. Once the aroma reaches the hypothalamus, the resulting stimulation propagates through the circulatory glands, eventually reaching the hippocampus—a crucial component composed of matter necessary for memory retention. It facilitates the body's response to the therapeutic properties of the fragrance via the practice of aromatherapy. In an alternate approach, if one were to blend the intrinsic oils derived from botanical sources with a suitable medium and administer them externally onto the skin surface, they would undergo absorption and subsequently facilitate the embodiment of the plants' distinct characteristics. One instance of this can be observed when employing tea tree oil as a means to diminish and eradicate toenail fungus, given its properties as an anti-fungal agent.

Aromatherapy refers to the utilization of natural essential oils derived from various parts of plants, such as bark, flowers, stems, leaves, and roots, with the objective of enhancing both physical and psychological wellness. The scent of those essential oils is widely believed to have a stimulating effect on cognitive functions. It is possible for essential oils to be absorbed transdermally, enabling their circulation through the bloodstream to potentially facilitate comprehensive healing of the body. The concept of integrative medicine refers to the combination of conventional methods with holistic approaches to achieve comprehensive healing throughout the entire body.

Aromatic botanical specimens and blossoms represent some of the most exquisite marvels orchestrated by the natural world. Through the course of extensive planetary evolution, the emergence of flowers paved the way for the exponential proliferation of life forms, resulting in the creation of the habitat we currently inhabit. In contemporary societies, fragrances derived from flowers, leaves, seeds, roots, and forests hold great importance, serving as integral components in various realms such as medicine, culinary practices, aromatic essences, culinary enhancements, and vibrant pigments.

The primary therapeutic benefit commonly associated with essential oils pertains to the practice of aromatherapy. The medical significance of unadulterated herbs and flowers is beyond dispute, supported by research findings, as is the therapeutic value of essential oils, which exhibit crucial healing properties. Certain oils have a cognitive effect on an individual's brain, and a number of essential oils possess antibacterial attributes, thereby mitigating the potential risk of a specific ailment when topically applied.

Appropriately administered dosages of medicinal essential oils prescribed by a certified physician have the potential to become more prevalent in the United States. While this practice is already happening in certain European medical contexts, it remains relatively uncommon in America. Individuals would be wise to refrain from utilizing essential oils if advised to do so by an individual lacking professional expertise, and instead seek guidance from a qualified aromatherapist possessing clinical training.

Multiple research studies have substantiated the efficacy of particular essential oils employed within the framework of aromatherapy clinics, namely rosemary and lavender, in facilitating relaxation for individuals experiencing heightened levels of stress or anxiety. The aroma of chamomile is widely believed to exert a nearly ubiquitous tranquilizing influence, resulting in a reduction of stimulation to the sympathetic nervous system, responsible for the fight or flight response and physiological symptoms such as perspiring hands or an escalated heart rate.

Essential Oils

Incorporating essential oils into your daily routine can yield numerous advantages. With a history spanning centuries, ample evidence exists documenting the myriad advantages and potential uses of essential oils. Every essential oil possesses distinct characteristics that render them appropriate for varied applications.

The plant-derived oils have been linked to possessing detoxifying, mood-enhancing, and invigorating characteristics. Throughout history, ancient civilizations have consistently utilized these indispensable oils as therapeutic solutions. The phenomenon is gaining popularity as practitioners of aromatherapy incorporate essential oils to offer alternative or complementary approaches to address a wide range of medical conditions. With many modern medicines to blame for worsening health problems, its little wonder why the trend is constantly picking up.

What Are Essential Oils?

Aromatic botanicals encompass volatile compounds which retain these vital oils. Present within the glandular structures of plants, these micro-droplets are responsible for imbuing each plant with its distinctive scent. After traversing the glands via diffusion, they disperse throughout the plant and emanate into the atmosphere, emitting an aromatic scent. In the case of a plant that produces fruits, these molecules significantly contribute to the taste profile of the fruit. These oils are commonly known as volatile essential oils, given their propensity to vaporize upon exposure to atmospheric conditions.

While it may not be deemed economically viable to extract essential oils from every aromatic plant, there are still more than 400 essential oils currently being produced.

Each oil is designated with a name that corresponds to the specific plant from which it is derived. The aroma of the oil intensifies and grows more robust with the passage of time as a tree reaches maturity. However, it should be noted that younger plants exhibit a propensity for generating a greater quantity of oils compared to their aged counterparts. From a visual perspective, one can discern the distinction between the two based on their color and viscosity, as the oils that have undergone further development and maturation tend to exhibit a deeper hue and a denser, resinous quality. Therefore, pure essential oils exhibit insolubility in water.

The plant oils exhibit hydrophobicity and thus do not readily combine with water. The inherent volatility of these substances can be effectively mitigated through the process of combining them with carrier oils. This serves to augment their capability in permeating the skin upon application through rubbing.

Overview of the Cardiac Chakra
Position: The Heart Chakra is situated precisely in the middle of the chest, in close proximity to the heart.
Color Attribute: It is obliquely connected with the hue green, which embodies the essence of the natural world.
Sangkrit: It is referred to as Anahata in the Sangkrit tradition.
Fundament and Obligation: The primary essence of the Heart Chakra lies in love and its transformative potential for healing. It exhibits a state that lies at the intersection of the physical and the spiritual realms, wherein the perception of sensations manifests as emotions such as love, hate, forgiveness, or harboring

resentments. Additionally, it encompasses the realization of engaging in acts of kindness and fostering connections with others.

Yoga Asana and Affirmation: The yogic posture corresponding to this specific chakra entails assuming the camel pose by reclining on your back, enabling the heart chakra to be exposed to illuminating energy and connect with the surrounding environment. The prescribed method for activating this particular Chakra involves bringing the index finger and thumb of your dominant hand in close proximity at the center of your chest, followed by replicating this action with your non-dominant hand, placing it gently on your left knee. Its inclination towards crystal is closely reminiscent of green jade, emerald, or aventurine. The potency of the color green promotes the harmonious circulation of energy within the Heart Chakra.

There are certain indicators that can assist in discerning whether your Heart

Chakra maintains equilibrium. If one is, then one shall discern indications of affection and empathy, gratitude, acceptance, and inner tranquility. It is possible for you to derive satisfaction from your current activities without experiencing undue stress or pressure.

When a disruption occurs in the flow of your Chakra, you may experience feelings of intolerance, resentment, confusion, distrust towards both your loved ones and yourself.

Excessive indicators manifest in the form of jealousy, which tends to arise when you consistently engage in excessive acts of selflessness and kindness, potentially allowing others to exploit or take advantage of you for their personal gain. Exhibiting kindness is a virtuous act, and committing benevolent actions is morally right. Nevertheless, excessive dedication can result in the erosion of one's own identity and the prioritization of others over oneself.

Engage in various activities that can facilitate the healing process of your blocked Heart Chakra, resulting in its reopening and restoration of balance. Immersing yourself in natural environments or being surrounded by vibrant greenery can be particularly effective. Additionally, spending quality time with children and animals can also contribute to the healing of your heart, as they possess an inherent energy of innocence that can be nurturing. Furthermore, cultivating plants has the potential to foster a sense of generosity within your heart, encouraging its sustained healing. The symbolism of green representing the heart in the Chakras system implies that it embodies the extent of our innate generosity. Consequently, maintaining a connection with the color green facilitates unhindered and joyful energy flow within the chest region. Incorporate green vegetables, such as broccoli, lettuce, and cabbage, into your diet to enhance your overall well-being and strengthen the Heart Chakra.

An Elucidation On The 7 Primary Chakras

As previously discussed, the human body comprises seven primary chakras. In the forthcoming chapter, our examination will encompass not just their spatial arrangement and correlation with physical well-being, but also their influential role in bolstering our psychological and emotional welfare.

The Root Chakra

The initial item on our inventory is the Root Chakra, which falls under the realm of the Earth Element. This particular energy center is referred to as such due to its designated function. Its objective is to establish a connection and establish a profound bond with the Earth, much like the way trees do. The Root is situated at the fundament of the spinal column.

The Root Chakra pertains to our fundamental requirements for survival, such as security, nourishment, and shelter. This focal point of energy embodies inquiries such as: To what extent do I experience security within this realm? Have all of my needs been fulfilled in this world? To what extent can I effectively adapt and prosper within the realms of this world? Inquiries pertaining to survival and safety fall within the jurisdiction of the First Chakra. Should you respond in the negative to these inquiries, it would indicate a deficiency in establishing a solid groundwork for one's existence.

An inequity or obstruction in the functioning of this chakra presents a significant challenge. Consider the scenario of possessing an exquisitely designed residence that is compromised by a structurally unsound base. It will falter before long. In order to provide further clarity, the following are the principal attributes of the Root:

Safety and security
Grounding
Physical identity
Basic needs

The designated hue of this chakra is crimson in accordance with official doctrine.

The Sacral Chakra

Originality, sentiments, and sensuousness - these are the fundamental principles of the Sacral Chakra. Within the aquatic element, the Sacral chakra facilitates our dynamic and adaptable nature. If the Root chakra is governed by our necessities, this particular chakra is governed by our enjoyment.

Situated at a distance of three inches below the navel, it extends towards the region encompassing our reproductive organs, namely the ovaries in women and the testicles in men. In terms of the physical aspect, it is interconnected with our lymphatic system. This energetic focal point embodies inquiries such as: How do you manifest your self-expression? How adept are you at navigating periods of reduced creative output?

The focal point of contention lies in this notion: the second chakra is the pivotal center that bestows upon us the ability to perceptibly experience the realm surrounding us. Through the utilization of our sensory faculties, the Sacral chakra elucidates a continuous flow of sentiments, innovative expression, and gratification. To put it differently, this constitutes the essence of our emotions. This energy hub serves to facilitate our adaptability in navigating diverse life circumstances by instilling a sense of malleability to our cognitive and affective processes. The behavioral attributes of this energy center can be described as follows:

Our ability to relate
Sensuality
Expressions of sexuality
How we engross ourselves in elaborate imagery
Our creativity
How can we establish our own autonomous realm
Perceiving the external environment

The hue affiliated with this particular chakra is orange, which is symbolically representative of creativity.

The Solar Plexus Chakra

It is unsurprising that the Solar Plexus chakra is governed by our power and intellect. Ultimately, this phenomenon is propelled by the elemental force of fire, which conveys the notion of thermal energy and the unswerving radiance of the sun. It can be found in the region known as the solar plexus, which encompasses the space between the chest and the navel.

The Solar Plexus Chakra is intricately linked to our gastrointestinal system, particularly the gastric sphere and the pancreatic region. This is attributed to the fact that it is the region of the human body responsible for the digestion and assimilation of food, ultimately serving as our primary source of energy. Attending to this vital energy center also promotes the well-being of the pancreas and enhances metabolic functions, particularly in the realm of carbohydrate processing. This energy center symbolizes inquiries such as: Have you successfully attained your objectives? What impedes you from reaching your utmost aspirations? In the event of a demanding circumstance, will you assume a position of leadership or retreat out of trepidation?

To conclude, it can be inferred that the Solar Plexus Chakra is intrinsically linked to one's determination, cognitive abilities, and capacity to progress and accomplish objectives. The manner in which you exhibit self-assertion, ambition, and determination is also contingent upon this particular energy center. Will you let the world control you or will you take the wheel?

Please find the behavioral attributes pertaining to the Solar Plexus Chakra listed below:

Will
Personal power
Displaying confidence in the presence of others or when confronted with a challenging situation
Assigning intentions/goals
The method of computing objects
Our "Warrior Energy"

The color of this chakra is yellow, as it is commonly linked to the element of fire.

The Heart Chakra

The fundamental principle upheld by the fourth chakra is affection, empathy, and embracing oneself and others. This principle is closely associated with the element of air. At a more profound level, the Heart Chakra serves as the conduit linking the material realm to the metaphysical realm; hence, it is propelled by the principle of integration. The energy center in question is positioned directly in the middle of the chest; however, it has been contended by certain authorities that its actual location is slightly to the left of the physical heart organ.

In terms of physicality, the fourth chakra is intricately linked to the heart and lungs, as they are predominantly reliant on the presence of air for their optimal functioning. Furthermore, it is intricately connected to the thymus gland, an organ that assumes responsibility for the regulation of our immune system. This energy center symbolizes inquiries such as: In what manner can I maintain a compassionate disposition? Have I already come to terms with the situation? Have I extended forgiveness to those who have committed wrongdoings against me? Any matters pertaining to affection, empathy, inclusion, and pardon are fundamentally grounded in the Heart chakra.

The fourth energetic center also serves to harmonize the lower chakras with the upper chakras. It serves as a conduit, connecting the domains of the physical realm and the realms that address our spiritual needs. The absence of the heart would result in a division of these two dimensions. It is imperative to acknowledge that the concept of love as it pertains to this specific energetic nexus is not necessarily limited to physical or sexual expressions of affection. It pertains to that transcendental love, that love that surpasses our self-centeredness and desires.

For the purpose of enhanced clarity, the subsequent information outlines the behavioral attributes associated with the fourth chakra:

Love
Empathy
Acceptance
Compassion
Forgiveness
Connecting with others
Connecting with one's self
Integration
Harmony in living

The hue linked to this chakra is green.

www.ingramcontent.com/pod-product-compliance
Lightning Source LLC
Chambersburg PA
CBHW050240120526
44590CB00016B/2172